PULMONOLOGY FOR KIDS
Respiratory System and
anatomy Book f

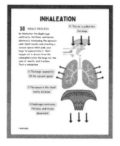

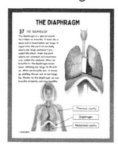

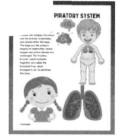

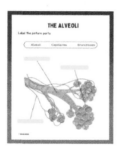

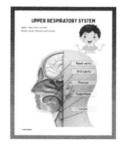

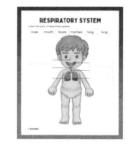

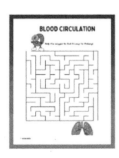

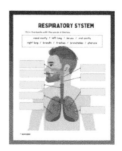

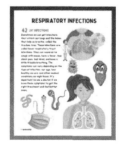

Contents

breathe

This Book Belongs to:

_____

for Kids

Respiratory system

H₂O

LUNGS

Have you ever wondered where the air you breathe goes inside your body? Well, it goes straight into your lungs! Your lungs are like two big, soft balloons inside your chest. When you take a breath, the air goes through your nose or mouth, down into your lungs.

Lungs have a unique shape like two large, fluffy sponges inside our chest. When fully inflated, they look like big balloons. Just like balloons, they can expand and contract as we breathe.

Your lungs are amazing organs that help you breathe and give your body the oxygen it needs to stay alive!

BREATHING

1 THE AIR

There is air everywhere around us. Air is something we can feel but cannot see. The wind is the air that is moving. The balloon is filled with air. You notice air when the trees' leaves rustle or blow in the wind. You can fly your kite due to the moving air. You blow up balloons with your mouth, to fill them with air.

2 BREATHING

Every day, we breathe throughout the day and night. We breathe in and out about 22,000 times a day. Most of the time, we move around without realising that we're breathing. Even when you're sleeping, you're still breathing. While sleeping, you breathe slowly and regularly. However, when you are dreaming, your breathing rate increases. The act of breathing is called respiration.

3 WHY DO YOU BREATHE?

To survive, every part of your body requires a gas called oxygen(O_2). All cells in your body use oxygen to produce energy. This energy is used to perform different activities like playing, moving, or even just thinking. Even when you are at rest and doing nothing, your body organs still need the energy to function properly. Your heart is constantly beating, your brain is continuously active, and most of the internal organs need energy and oxygen continuously. As a result, Oxygen is essential for your life

4 BREATHING IN AND OUT

When the body uses oxygen to produce energy, a gas called carbon dioxide(Co_2) is produced as a waste product. You breathe in to provide your body with oxygen and breathe out to get rid of the waste gas, carbon dioxide. Breathing in is called inspiration, or inhaling. Breathing out is called expiration, or exhaling.

5 RESPIRATORY SYSTEM

The network of organs that helps in breathing is called the respiratory system. It consists of your, lungs, and airways which the air passes through. Together, these organs work to provide the body with oxygen and eliminate waste gases like carbon dioxide. The main organs in your respiratory system are the lungs.

They are on each side of your heart, inside your chest cavity, and protected by the rib cage.

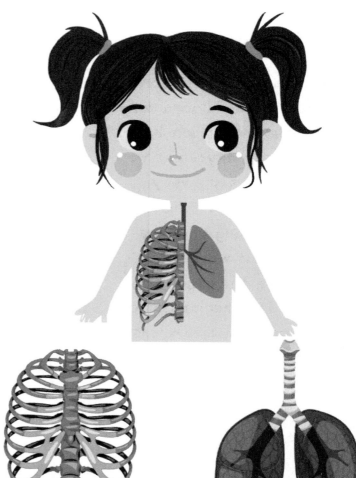

6 HUMANS HAVE TWO LUNGS

The human lungs are a pair of spongy organs located on either side of the chest cavity. Not only humans but all mammals also have lungs. Mammals are animals with backbones and have glands that produce milk to feed young offspring. For example, dogs, cows, cats, horses, sheep, monkeys, bears, lions, and rats.

Although humans and these animals appear different, their lung anatomy is pretty similar.

7 ONE LUNG ONLY

Not all animals have the same lung structure as humans' lungs. For example, snakes don't require as much oxygen as we do, so their lungs are very different from ours. Snakes only have one thin, long lung (the right lung) that works as a simple air sac. The other lung (left lung), is either absent or Shrieked to a tiny size and is known as a vestigial lung

8 GILLS INSTEAD OF LUNGS

All Fish must also take oxygen and release carbon dioxide in order to survive. However, they have gills instead of lungs. Fish heads have branching organs called gills that are filled with so many tiny blood vessels. Water flows over the fish's gills when it opens its mouth, allowing dissolved oxygen found in the water to be absorbed by the blood. Most aquatic animals, like squid, mollusk, octopus, shark, fish, and tadpoles have no lungs and breathe through gills instead.

9 INSECTS HAVE NO LUNGS .

There are also several species and creatures, such as ants, grasshoppers, bees, and houseflies, that have no lungs at all. All insects don't have lungs. To breathe, they have holes called spiracles on their body. Each spiracle is connected to a network of finely branching tubes known as tracheae. The tracheae spread throughout the body to deliver oxygen to every cell.

10 EARTHWORMS

Earthworms Worms, like us, breathe in oxygen and breathe out carbon dioxide, but they don't have lungs. They can't breathe through their mouths, instead, they breathe through their moist skin. The skin of a worm is covered in mucus, which keeps the skin moist and helps in oxygen absorption. This is why they prefer to stay underground most of the time and come to the surface after rain.

11 BREATHING IN HUMANS

Humans breathe through their lungs. When you inhale (breathe in), air rushes into the lungs, so they inflate like a balloon filled with air.

The oxygen from that air is transported to your bloodstream. Simultaneously, carbon dioxide, a waste gas, travels from your blood to your lungs and is exhaled (breathed out).

CIRCULATORY SYSTEM

Circle things that have lungs.

CIRCULATORY SYSTEM

Circle things that do not have lungs.

12 THE NOSE

Your nose is the first organ in your respiratory system. It is also the only visible part of the respiratory system that can be seen from the outside of your body. The nose serves as the respiratory system's air entrance point. It aids in shaping your appearance and giving your face its own contour. Your nose has two openings known as the nostrils, which, allow air to enter and exit the nasal cavities.

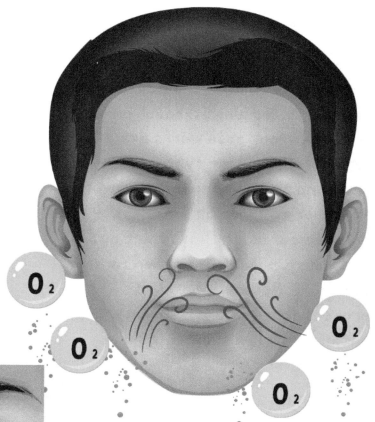

O₂ O₂ O₂ O₂ O₂

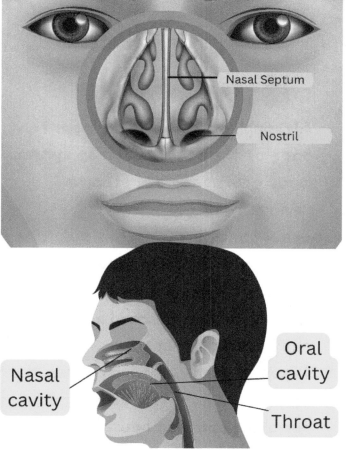

Nasal Septum

Nostril

Nasal cavity

Oral cavity

Throat

13 THE NASAL CAVITY

The nasal cavity is a large space in the middle of the face inside the nose. The nasal cavity is divided into two separate parts by the nasal septum. Each of these cavities is called a nasal passage. During breathing, air passes through these air passages. The nasal cavity is located above the roof of the mouth and curves down to join the throat at the back.

14 THE ULTIMATE AIR CLEANER

Air enters the respiratory system through the nose or the mouth, then travels to the lungs through a pathway. Your nose works as an ultimate air cleaner system. A mucus lining and tiny hairs in the nose work together to filter air before it enters your lungs. Hair filters out dirt, dust, pollen, and other foreign particles. Nose hair helps to prevent foreign objects from entering the lungs and causing infection.

15 TRIM NASAL HAIR

Although nose hair is an important part of the body's defense system, many adult people prefer to remove it to get a better appearance if it extends out from their nostrils. They should use a trimmer instead of tweezers. Too much nose hair removal may make the body more sensitive to many types of particles which enter the respiratory system with air. Hair removing can also cause irritation and infections.

16 NASAL BLOOD VESSELS

The moist, inner lining of the nose is called the mucosa. It is a type of tissue that contain glands that produce mucus. The nasal mucosa is richly supplied with blood vessels that are warmer than the air that is being inhaled. As a result, the heat is transferred from the blood vessels to the air passing over them and the air becomes warmer. This is an important process to protect the respiratory system from cold air, which can be harmful to the sensitive tissues of the lungs

17 SENSE OF SMELL

Your nasal cavity contains olfactory receptors, which are specialized nerve endings that allow you to detect and identify different smells. Smelling helps us to detect and avoid polluted air by noticing specific odors. For example, smelling gasoline, smoke, or other chemical odors may indicate the presence of pollutants in the air that could be harmful to our health. . Our brains recognize these odors and initiate a reflexive response, such as coughing or holding our breath.

18 THE MUCUS

The mucus in your nose is more than just a slimy and slippery substance; it serves a purpose. It filters the air by trapping and killing bacteria, germs, and other particles, keeping them out of your lungs. Mucus also helps to lubricate the nasal passages, keeping them moist and comfortable. Also, mucus contains antibodies that help to protect the body from infections so it helps to remove irritants and allergens from the air, reducing the risk of respiratory problems.

BL⬤⬤D

19 THE NOSEBLEEDS

The mucus in your nose keeps your nose moist, preventing nosebleeds caused by a dry nose. During a nosebleed, blood flows from one or both nostrils. It can occur when one of the blood vessels in the nose's lining bursts. A dry nose, dry climate, or nose picking can all cause nosebleeds. It is common in children and is usually not serious, but it can be annoying. Sit down and firmly pinch the soft part of your nose, just above your nostrils, for at least 10-15 minutes to stop a nosebleed.

NASAL CAVITY

Color things that are found inside the nose green.

Lips

Mucus

Hair

Mucosa

Nail

Blood vessel

Eyelash

Septum

Teeth

NASAL CAVITY

Write or draw things inside the nose that can filter and warmth the air before it reaches the lungs

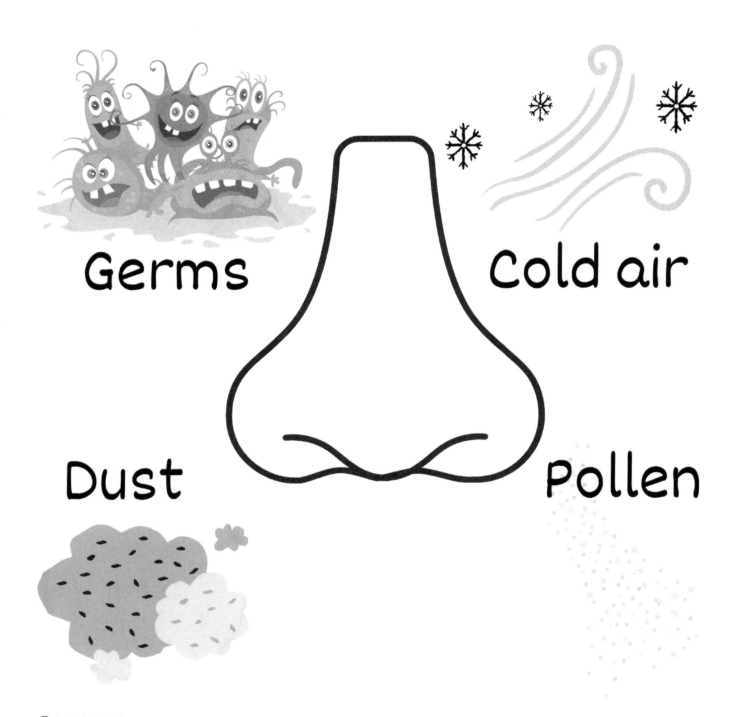

Germs

Cold air

Dust

Pollen

NASAL CAVITY

Color the functions of the nasal cavity.

Warming the air

Mixing food

Swallowing

Move the body

Filtering the air

Catching germs

Moisten the air

Digesting food

Protect the lungs

THROAT

20 THE PHARYNX

The pharynx, or throat, is an important part of the respiratory system. It is a muscular tube that runs from the back of the nose and mouth to the voice box. It serves as an air passageway during respiration. It has small hair called cilia that help filter out dust, dirt, and other particles that may pass through the nasal cavity. Furthermore, it contains glands that produce mucus to moisten and clean the respiratory tract. It helps air go in and out of your lungs and helps the food go down to your stomach.

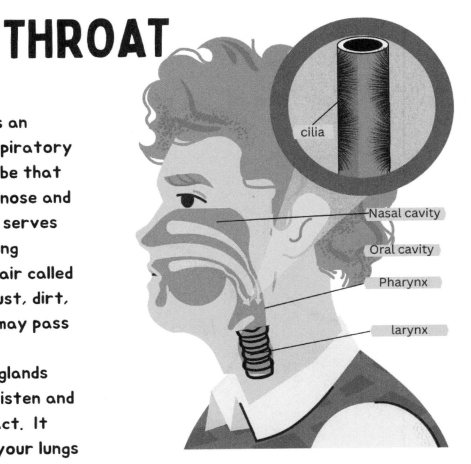

cilia

Nasal cavity

Oral cavity

Pharynx

larynx

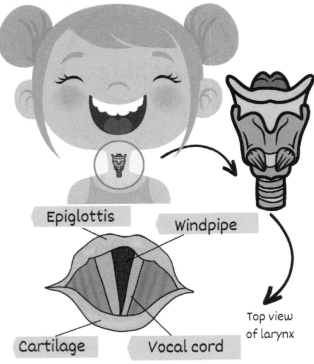

Epiglottis

Windpipe

Cartilage

Vocal cord

Top view of larynx

21 THE LARYNX

The larynx, also known as the voice box, is located in the neck. It is important for both breathing and sound production. It is made up of a strong C-shaped tissue called cartilage which keeps the larynx open. The larynx regulates the flow of air and helps in producing sounds when we speak. Larynx also has a small flap called the epiglottis. The epiglottis' main function is to prevent food and liquids from entering the windpipe when we swallow.

PHARYNX   VS   LARYNX

- The pharynx extends from the nasal cavity and mouth to the larynx. It is also called the throat.

- Both air and food pass through the pharynx.

- The walls of the pharynx are made of muscles

- The pharynx is involved in both digestion and respiration. It delivers food to the esophagus and air to larynx.

- It is a part of both the respiratory and digestive system

- larynx is the upper portion of the trachea. It is also called the vocal box since it contains vocal cords.

- The air only enters the larynx

- The wall of the larynx is made up of cartilage.

- The larynx is involved in breathing, producing sound, and preventing the inhalation of food, liquids, and other materials.

- It is a part of the respiratory system only.

RESPIRATION

Match with the correct organ

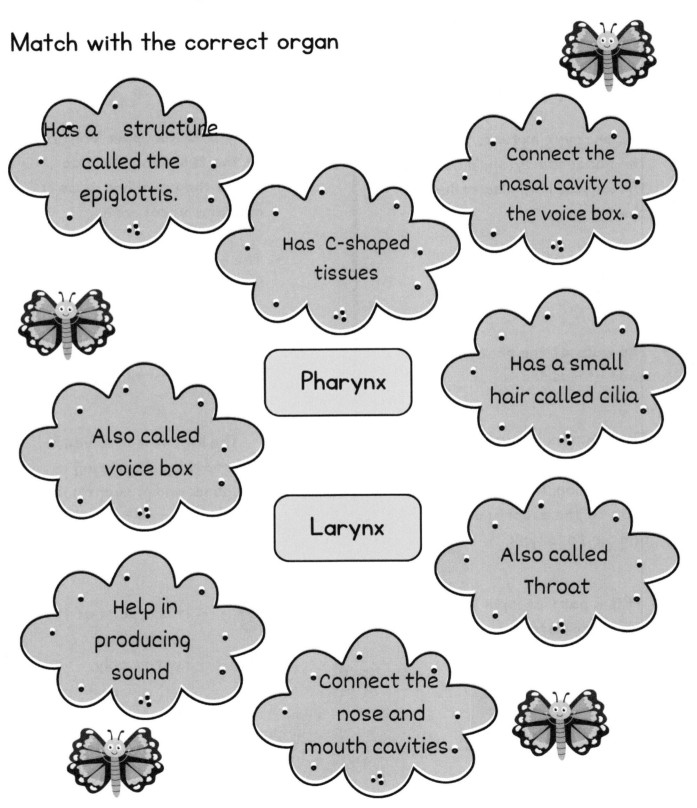

Has a structure called the epiglottis.

Has C-shaped tissues

Connect the nasal cavity to the voice box.

Pharynx

Has a small hair called cilia

Also called voice box

Larynx

Also called Throat

Help in producing sound

Connect the nose and mouth cavities.

THE SINUSES

23 THE SINUSES.

The sinuses are a collection of air-filled spaces located within the face and skull bones. Their primary function is to reduce the weight of the skull. They are lined with mucous membranes. The sinuses are connected to the inside of the nose via small openings known as Ostia. The mucus helps to moisten and filter the air that enters the nose.

24 THE SINUSES LOCATION

There are four main groups of sinuses:

- The frontal sinuses, (located above the eyes and behind both eyebrows).
- The maxillary sinuses(located in the structure of the cheekbones).
- The ethmoid sinuses(located at both sides of the nose, up by the bridge).
- The sphenoid sinuses (located behind the nose, and directly in front of the brain).

25 THE SINUSES FUNCTION

To keep the nose clean, the sinuses produce thin mucus that drains from the nose. Sinuses are normally filled with air, but when they become blocked and filled with fluid, bacteria or germs can grow and cause a sinus infection, also known as sinusitis. Sinus infections are also caused by viruses, allergies, fever, or structural issues in the nasal septum.

26 SYMPTOMS OF SINUSITIS

Sinus problems can be painful because they cause inflammation and pressure in the sinus cavities. the patient might feel certain things like :

- Headache especially in the brow or around the eyes
- Trouble breathing through a blocked or stuffy nose.
- Sense of smell or taste loss
- Face pain, especially around the eyes, cheeks, or forehead

27 REMEDIES FOR SINUSITIS

There are several tips you can do at home for treating sinus infections. Some examples are:

- Drinking plenty of water.
- Rinsing the nasal cavity with a saline solution.
- Inhaling steam and use a special spray made of salt and water.
- Take a hot shower or use a humidifier at your room.

28 SINUSITIS MEDICATIONS.

Sinus infections can make you uncomfortable but doctors can help you feel better. Here's how they might help:

1. If the infection is caused by bacteria, the doctor might give you antibiotics.
2. To make your nose feel less swollen the doctor might give you a special spray made of salt and water.
3. To help with a headache or face pain, the doctor might give you Painrelife.

THE SINUSES

Color with the correct color

- The maxillary sinuses(in the cheekbones)

- The sphenoid sinuses(behind the nose)

- The ethmoid sinuses (at sides of the nose)

- The frontal sinuses (above the eyes)

THE SINUSES

Draw and color the four sets of sinuses in their correct place.

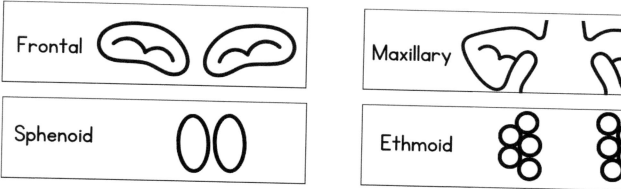

Frontal

Maxillary

Sphenoid

Ethmoid

THE SINUSES

Anna has a painful headache in her forehead because she suffers from a sinus infection. Write or draw three things that she can do to feel better.

THE SINUSES

Mark with a tick the clouds that show any symptoms of sinusitis

Blocked nose

Hair losses

Diarrhea

Forehead Headache

Skin irritation

Facial pain

Reduced sense of smell

Stomach pain

UPPER RESPIRATORY SYSTEM

29 UPPER RS

The upper respiratory system is the first part of the respiratory system that is located above the lungs. The nose, sinuses, pharynx, and larynx are all part of the upper respiratory system. The main function of the upper respiratory system is to filter, warm, and humidify the air that is breathed in. This is done by the nose and sinuses. Then direct the air to the lungs while preventing any food, liquid, or other substances from entering the lungs. This is done by the pharynx and larynx.

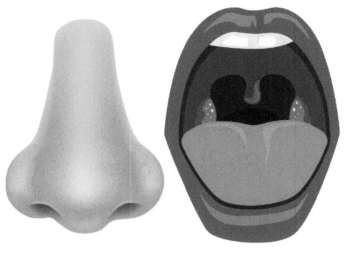

Filter

Warm

Humidify

Air

UPPER RESPIRATORY SYSTEM

Upper respiratory system
(Nasal cavity, Pharynx and larynx)

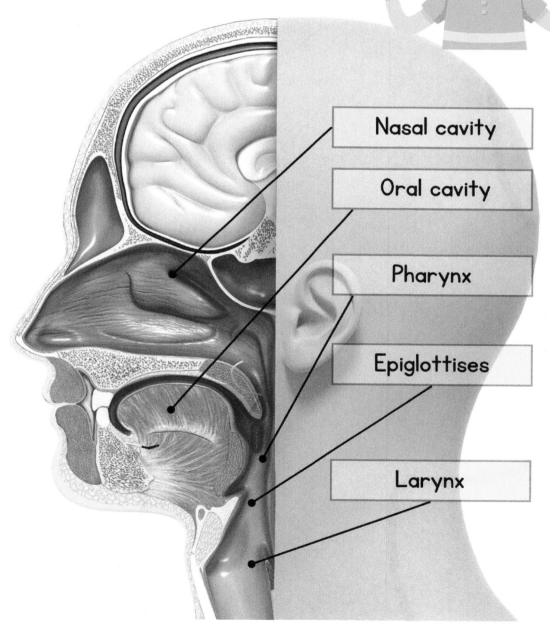

Nasal cavity

Oral cavity

Pharynx

Epiglottises

Larynx

UPPER RESPIRATORY SYSTEM

DRAW & LABEL The Upper RS parts

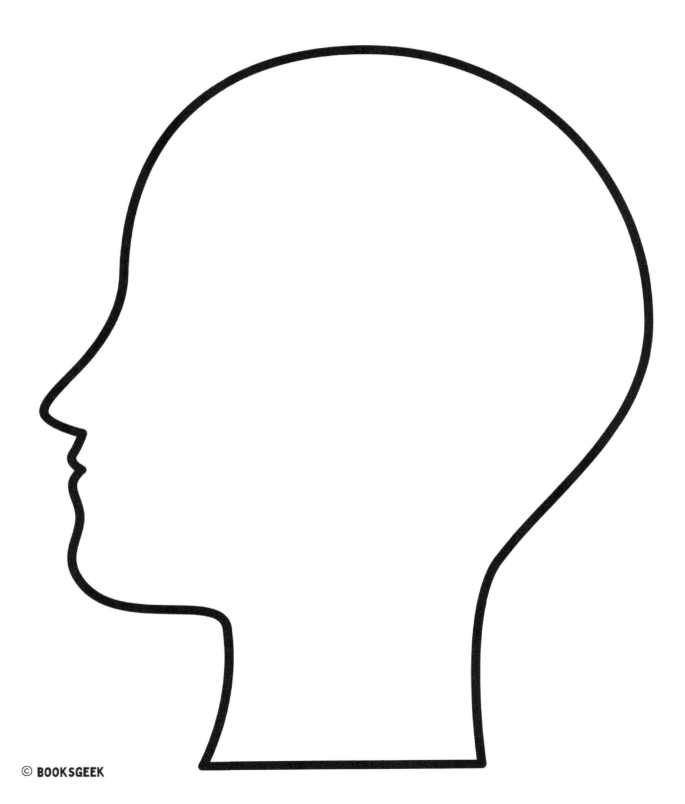

UPPER RESPIRATORY SYSTEM

Find the words below

```
S  I  T  T  O  T  O  L  G  I  P  E
Z  O  E  X  E  S  O  N  P  P  M
Y  T  I  V  A  C  I  B  M  P
K  W  L  X  N  Y  R  A  L  H
E  X  O  F  S  H  A  V  R  A
V  C  I  L  I  A  P  B  B  R
G  P  S  M  U  T  P  E  S  Y
S  U  C  U  M  C  K  U  V  N
N  O  S  T  R  I  L  S  E  X
F  V  T  V  I  S  U  N  I  S
```

WORD BANK

- cavity
- cilia
- mucus
- epiglottis
- sinus
- larynx
- septum
- pharynx
- nose
- nostrils

UPPER RESPIRATORY SYSTEM

Color the bubbles that have words belong to the Upper Respiratory System

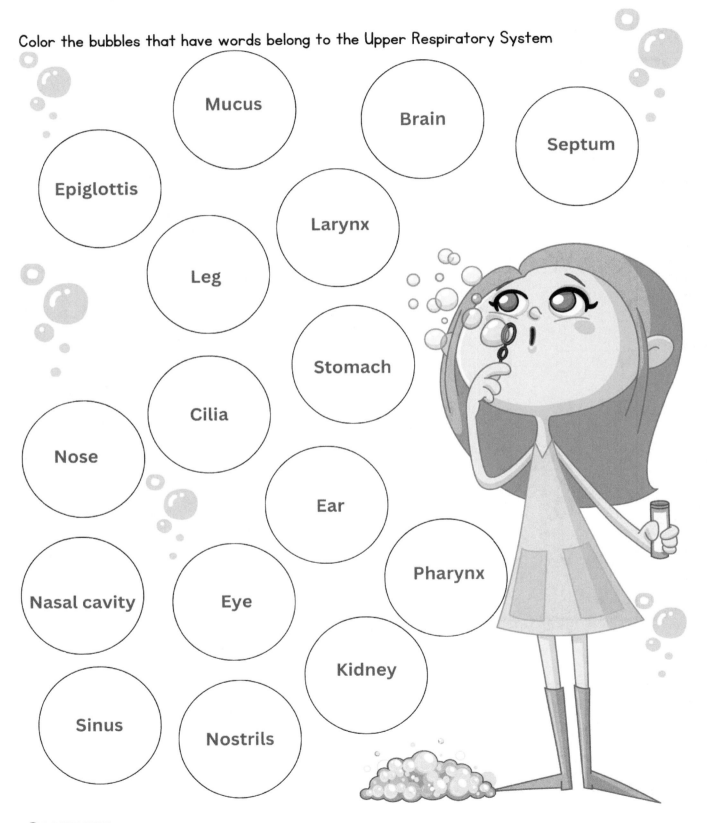

Mucus

Brain

Septum

Epiglottis

Larynx

Leg

Stomach

Cilia

Nose

Ear

Nasal cavity

Eye

Pharynx

Kidney

Sinus

Nostrils

THE TRACHEA

30 TRACHEA

The trachea, or windpipe, is a tube that connects the larynx (voice box) to the lungs. Its function is to transport air from the nose and mouth to the lungs for breathing. The trachea is made up of a series of rings called cartilages that help keep the trachea open. The tracheal wall is covered with small hair called cillia and mucus, which work together to trap foreign particles like dust and bacteria before they enter the lungs.

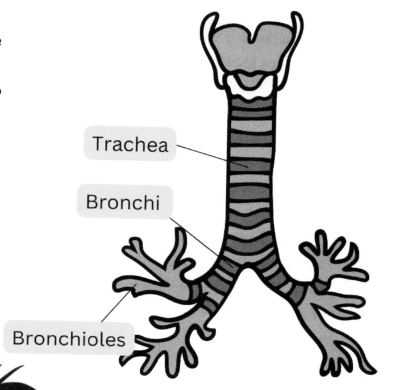

Trachea

Bronchi

Bronchioles

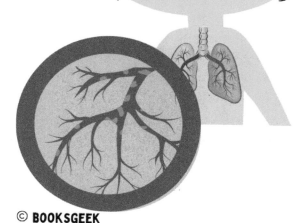

31 THE BRONCHI

The trachea divides into two branches called bronchi. Each bronchus (The singular of bronchi) enters one of the two lungs. These bronchi divide further into smaller and smaller branches called bronchioles, which lead to tiny air sacs inside the lungs called alveoli. The alveoli are where gas exchange between the lungs and the bloodstream occurs during the process of breathing.

THE ALVEOLI

32 ALVEOLI

The alveoli are tiny air sacs found in the lungs. They look like tiny balloons filled with air. They are the place where oxygen and carbon dioxide are exchanged.

The wall of the alveoli is extremely thin, which makes it easier to exchange gasses with the bloodstream. They are surrounded by tiny blood vessels (capillaries).

The alveoli and capillaries form a network that allows gases to exchange.

Cluster of alveoli

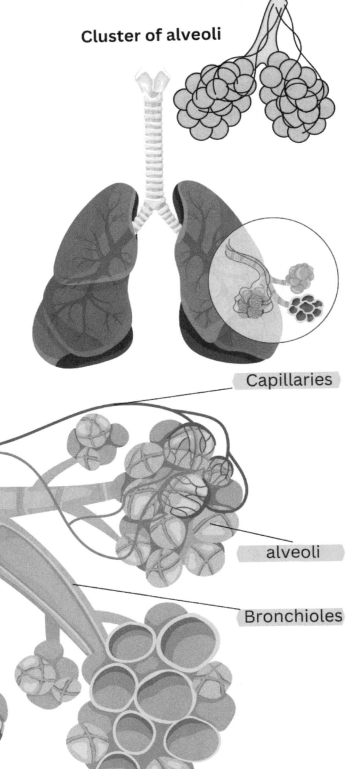

Capillaries

alveoli

Bronchioles

The alveoli are surrounded by network of tiny blood vessels called capillaries.

33 GASSES EXCHANGE

When we breathe, oxygen goes into our lungs and enters tiny air sacs called alveoli. From there, it moves into our blood through tiny blood vessels called capillaries. At the same time, carbon dioxide from our blood goes back into the alveoli. The oxygen-rich blood goes to our heart and is pumped to all the cells in our body. The blood with carbon dioxide goes back to the lungs and we breathe it out. This process keeps happening as long as we keep breathing!

The oxygen-rich blood goes to all the cells in our body. The blood with carbon dioxide goes back to the lungs and we breathe it out.

THE TRACHEA

Label the trachea parts.

Bronchi   Bronchioles   Trachea

THE ALVEOLI

Label the picture parts.

Alveoli   Capillaries   Bronchioles

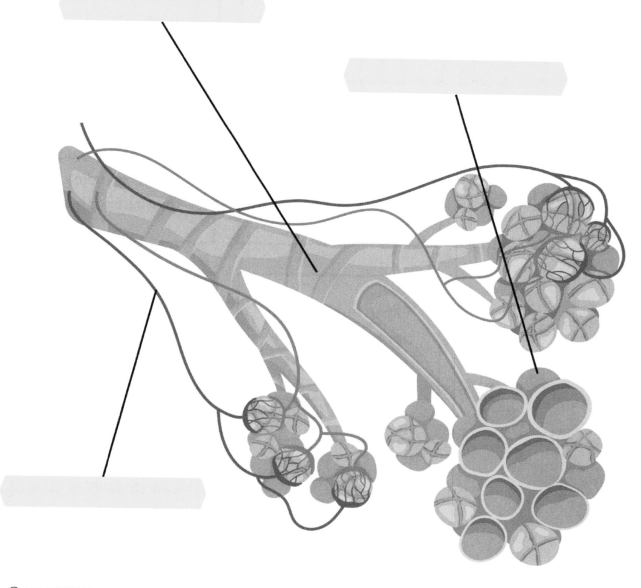

THE TRACHEA

Color with the correct color.

 Alveolus

 Trachea

Sac-like structures	Also called the windpipe	lined with cilia
connects the larynx to the lungs	Located inside the lungs	It is where oxygen and carbon dioxide are exchanged.

Filter out harmful particles from the air	Surrounded by capillaries
Lined with mucus	Divides into two branches

THE LUNGS

34 THE LUNGS ANATOMY AND SIZE

Your lungs are like pink sponges and they help you breathe. You have two lungs, one on each side of your chest. The lungs have different shapes. The right lung is wider and shorter because it has to make room for the liver on the right side. The left lung is longer and narrower because it is near the heart. Both lungs work together to let you breathe in fresh air and get rid of waste gases.

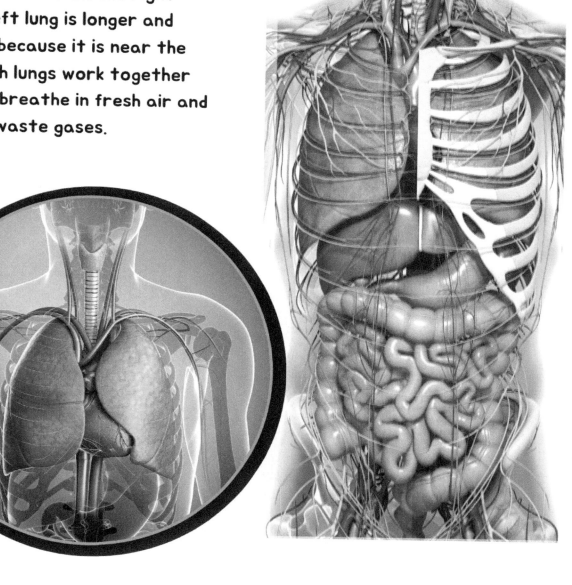

35 THE LUNG LOBES

The lungs are divided into different parts called lobes. The right lung has three lobes, while the left lung has two lobes. These lobes are like sections that help the lungs do their job. They are separated by deep grooves called fissures. The left lung has an upper and lower lobe, while the right lung has an upper, middle, and lower lobe. Between the lungs, there is a space, where the heart, trachea, and esophagus are located.

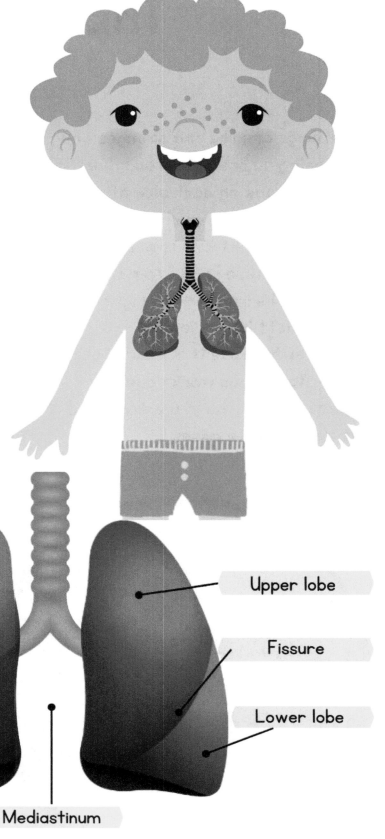

Upper lobe

Fissure

Middle lobe

Fissure

Lower lobe

Upper lobe

Fissure

Lower lobe

Mediastinum

36 MEDIASTINUM

The space in your chest, between your left and right lungs, is called the mediastinum. It is located in the middle section of your thoracic cavity. It contains the majority of the thoracic organs. The heart, great vessels, trachea, and essential nerves are all housed in the mediastinum and surrounded by connective tissue for additional protection.

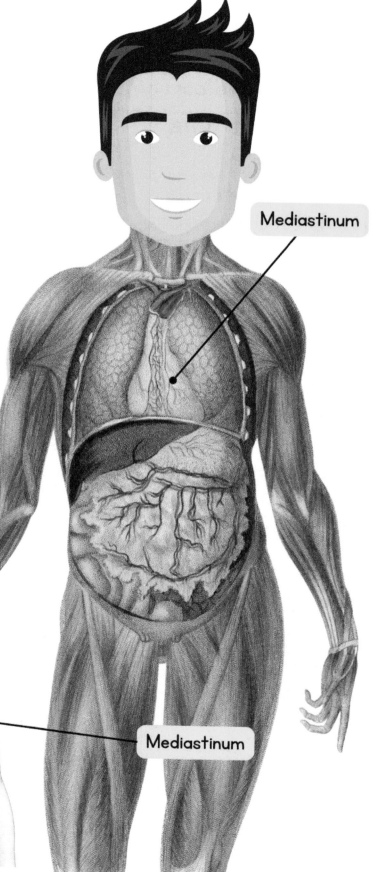

Mediastinum

Mediastinum

THE LUNGS

Color with the correct color.

Right lung	Left lung
● Upper lobe	● Upper lobe
● Middle lobe	● Lower lobe
● Lower lobe	

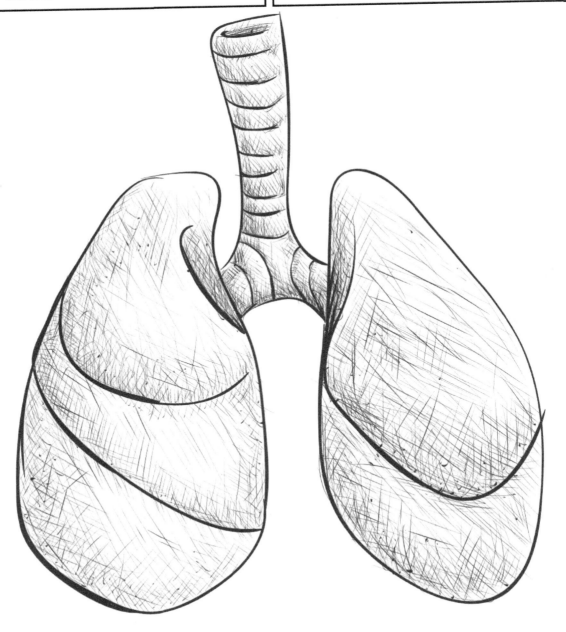

THE LUNGS

Color with the correct color.

 Right lung

 Left lung

The liver located just under it.	The heart is very close to it.
It has two lobes	It is shorter and wider than the other one.

It has three lobes	Located at the right side of chest cavity.	It is longer and narrower than the other one.
It has one fissure	It has two fissures .	Located at the left side of chest cavity.

THE LUNGS

Label the picture parts.

Bronchi   Lobe   Fissure   Trachea

Right lung   Left lung

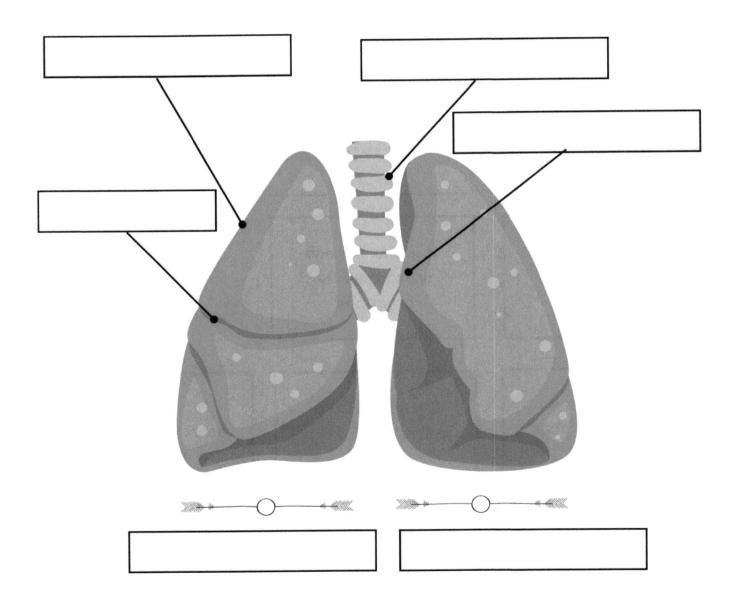

THE DIAPHRAGM

37 THE DIAPHRAGM

The diaphragm is a special muscle that helps us breathe. It looks like a dome and is found below our lungs. It separates the part of our body where our lungs and heart are, called the chest, from the part where our stomach and intestines are, called the abdomen. When we breathe in, the diaphragm moves down, allowing our lungs to fill with air. When we breathe out, it moves up, pushing the air out of our lungs. So, thanks to the diaphragm, we can breathe properly and stay healthy.

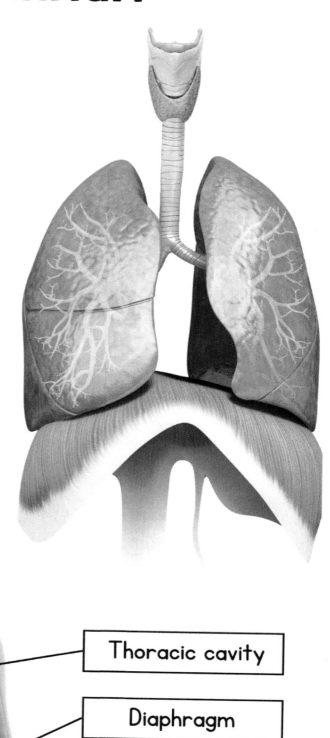

Thoracic cavity

Diaphragm

Abdominal cavity

INHALEATION

38 INHALE PROCESS

On inhalation the diaphragm contracts, flattens, and moves downward, increasing the space in your chest cavity and creating a vacuum space which pulls your lungs to expand into it. Rich-oxygen air is drawn from the atmosphere into the lungs via the nose or mouth, and trachea.. That is inhalation .

4- The air is pulled into the lungs

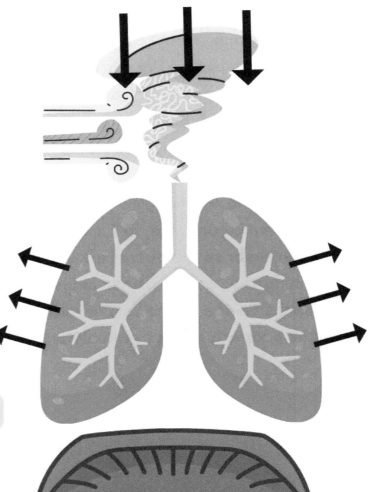

3-The lungs expand to fill the vacuum space

2-The space in the chest cavity increase.

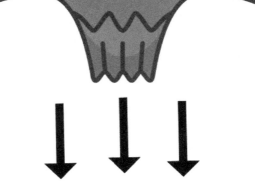

1-Diaphragm contracts, flattens, and moves downward.

EXHALEATION

39 EXHALE PROCESS

On exhalation , your diaphragm relaxes and moves up into your chest cavity, returning to its dome-like shape. As the space in your chest cavity shrinks, your lungs deflate,and get smaller forcing carbon dioxide-rich air out of your lungs and windpipe, and then out of your nose or mouth.

3-The lungs shrinks and get smaller.

2-The space in the chest cavity decrease.

1-Diaphragm relaxes and moves upwards.

4- carbon dioxide-rich air pushed out of the lungs

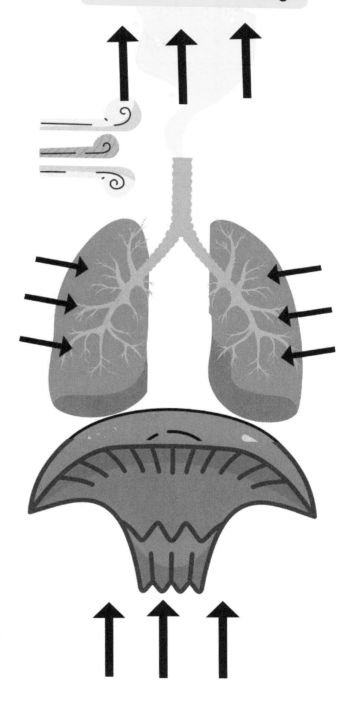

THE LUNGS

Label the picture parts.

Chest cavity	Abdominal cavity	Diaphragm
Right lung		Left lung

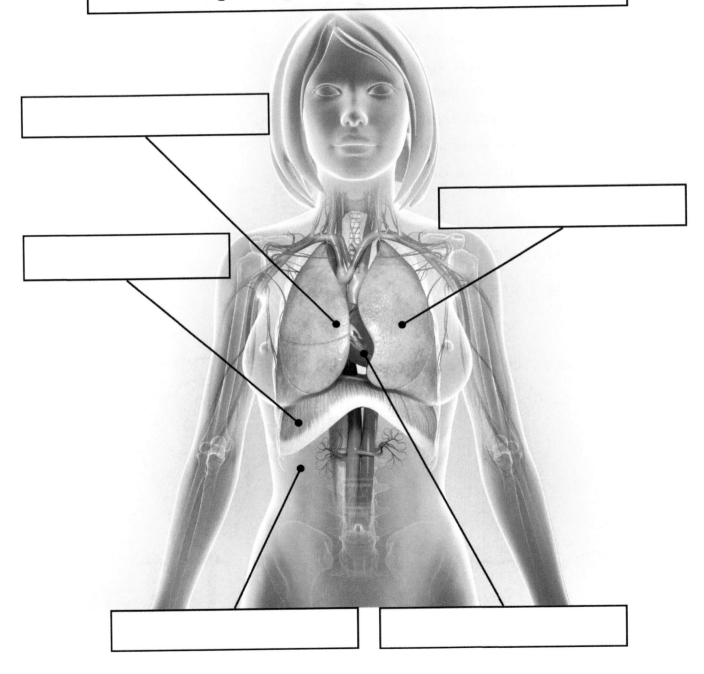

RESPIRATORY SYSTEM

Color with the correct color

- Trachea- red
- Right lung-blue
- Left lung-green
- Diaphragm- yellow
- Bronchi-purple

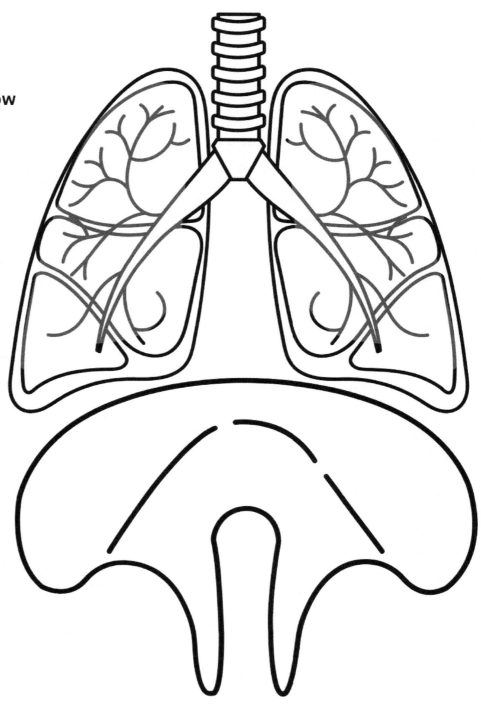

LOWER RESPIRATORY SYSTEM

40 LOWER RS

The lower respiratory tract includes the windpipe (trachea) and the bronchi, bronchioles, and alveoli within the lungs. The lungs are the primary organs of respiration, where oxygen and carbon dioxide are exchanged. The trachea, bronchi, and bronchioles together are called the bronchial tree, which transports air to and from the lungs.

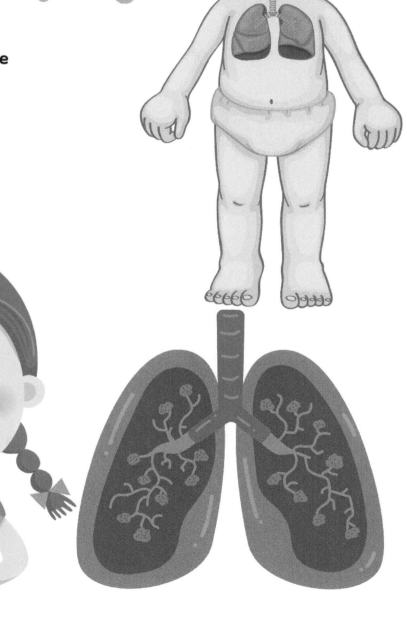

LOWER RESPIRATORY SYSTEM

The lower respiratory system tract includes the windpipe (trachea), the lungs, the bronchi, bronchioles, and alveoli.

Trachea

Bronchi

Bronchioles

Alveoli

Lung

LOWER RESPIRATORY SYSTEM

Find the words below

```
Z  M  N  E  G  H  L  S  E  B  O  L  P  S  Q
A  E  L  O  G  A  N  Y  R  G  V  B  A  F  M
F  P  Y  G  J  I  G  H  V  J  I  R  V  Z  X
X  J  U  L  L  E  Q  F  Q  F  M  O  C  T  X
A  E  H  C  A  R  T  Q  O  H  U  N  J  J  J
P  K  E  R  U  S  S  I  F  J  N  C  Q  N  B
C  Q  Y  R  B  L  T  G  O  F  I  H  I  Z  S
U  S  Y  A  W  R  I  A  U  S  T  I  G  S  U
E  K  T  G  U  F  O  C  H  G  S  M  X  C  T
P  H  I  T  C  W  K  P  Z  N  A  N  V  S  P
X  W  J  I  W  P  E  B  Z  U  I  K  J  B  U
U  A  L  V  E  O  L  I  H  L  D  N  E  H  Y
Y  R  A  L  L  I  P  A  C  D  E  F  E  V  Z
J  N  X  Z  O  O  F  L  T  S  M  Z  W  U  N
S  E  L  O  I  H  C  N  O  R  B  X  N  E  N
```

WORD BANK

- Lungs
- Fissure
- Trachea
- lobes
- mediastinum
- Alveoli
- Bronchi
- Bronchiole
- airways
- capillary

RESPIRATORY SYSTEM

Fill in the blanks with the words in the box.

nasal cavity / left lung / larynx / oral cavity

right lung / bronchi / trachea / bronchioles / pharynx

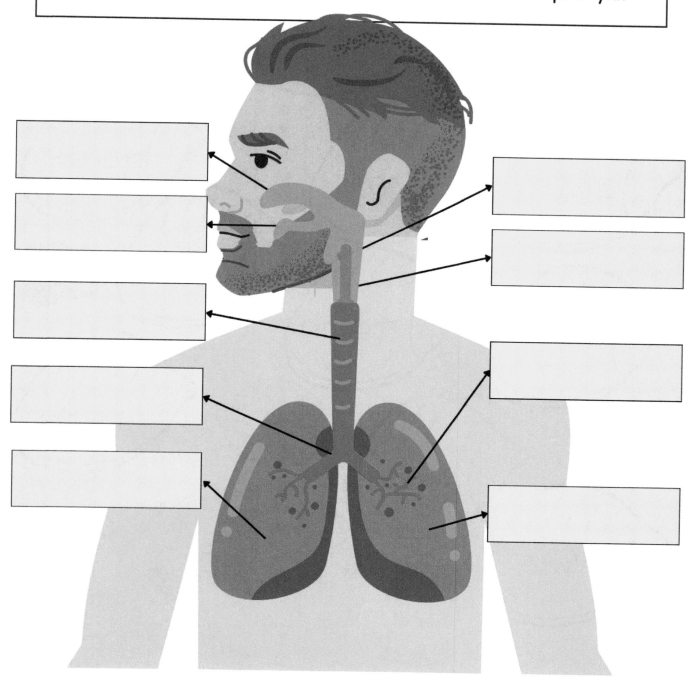

LOWER RESPIRATORY SYSTEM

Color the shells that have words belong to the lower Respiratory System.

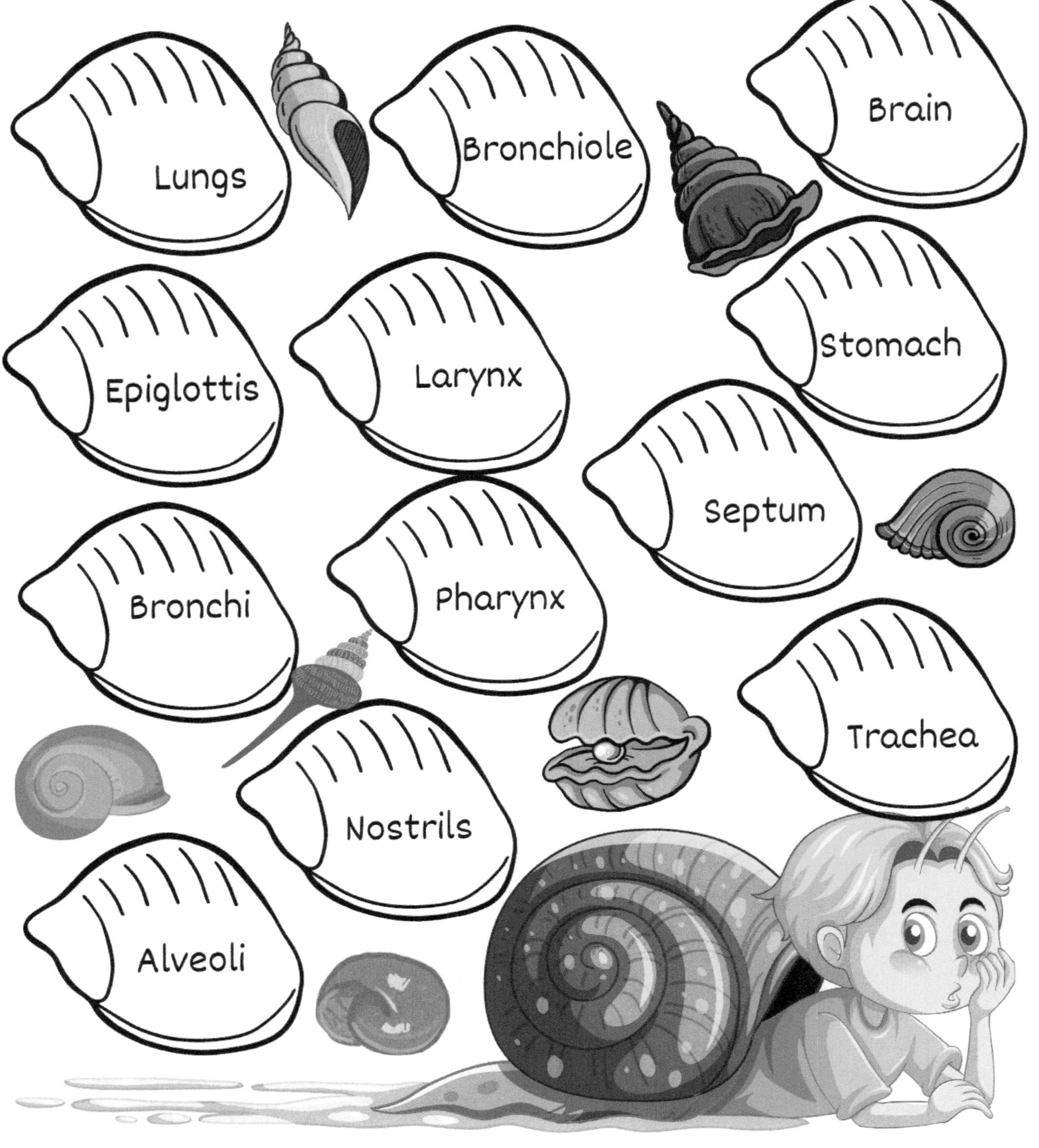

Lungs

Bronchiole

Brain

Epiglottis

Larynx

Stomach

Septum

Bronchi

Pharynx

Trachea

Nostrils

Alveoli

RESPIRATORY INFECTIONS

41 URT INFECTIONS

When we get sick, sometimes it affects the parts of our body involved in breathing, like our nose, sinuses, and throat. This is called an upper respiratory tract infection. It can make our nose runny or stuffy, give us a low-grade fever, make us cough, and cause a sore throat. We might feel pressure in our face and sinuses too. But don't worry, these infections are usually not serious and go away on their own in about a week or so. In the meantime, it's important to rest, drink plenty of warm liquids, and take care of ourselves.

RESPIRATORY INFECTIONS

42 LRT INFECTIONS

Sometimes we can get infections that affect our lungs and the tubes that help us breathe, called the trachea tree. These infections are called lower respiratory tract infections. They can cause us to cough with mucus, have a fever, feel chest pain, feel tired, and have a little trouble breathing. The symptoms can vary depending on the type of infection, our age, how healthy we are, and other medical conditions we might have. It's important to see a doctor if we have these symptoms to get the right treatment and feel better soon.

43 SORE THROAT

Sometimes when we have a cold or cough, we might also get a sore throat. It's a very common thing, especially for kids and teenagers, and even grown-ups can get it a few times a year. A sore throat can make it hurt or feel scratchy when we swallow or talk. But the good news is that it usually goes away on its own after a few days, especially if we rest, drink warm fluids, and take care of ourselves.

44 DRY COUGHING

When we have a respiratory infection, like a cold or flu, we might start coughing. Coughing is our body's way of getting rid of germs and irritants in our throat and lungs. Sometimes we have a dry cough, which means it doesn't produce mucus. It can feel like a tickle in our throat. This kind of cough is common with respiratory infections. Drinking warm fluids and taking rest can help soothe a cough.

45 WET COUGH AND FEVER

Sometimes when we have a respiratory infection, we might have a wet cough. This means that we cough up thick mucus from our lungs. It's called a productive cough because it helps clear our airways. A wet cough can be a sign of a lung infection or when our lungs fill with fluid, making it harder to breathe. Different germs like bacteria, viruses, or fungi can cause these infections. The color of the mucus can give us clues about the type of infection. Clear or white mucus is often from a virus, while yellow or green mucus can be from bacteria. The doctor will give us the right medicine and treatment depending on what's causing the cough.

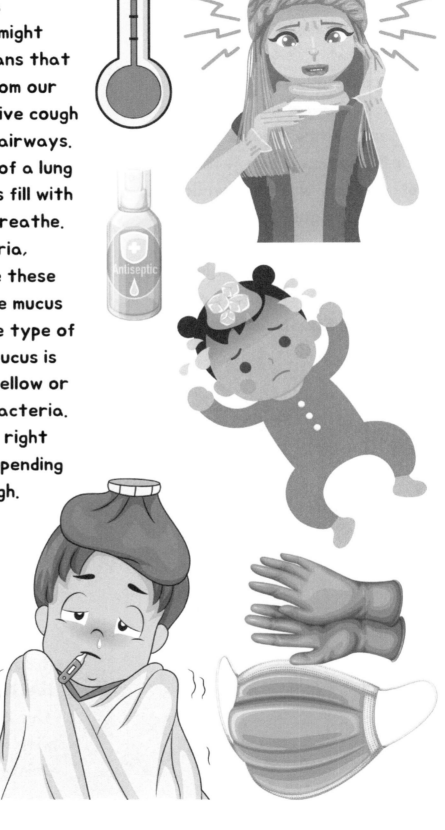

46 RUNNY OR STUFFY NOSE

When we catch a cold or have allergies, our nose can behave in different ways. Sometimes it becomes runny, and mucus flows out of our nose. Other times, it feels stuffy, making it hard to breathe through our nose. A runny nose happens when our body produces more mucus, which can be triggered by cold weather, colds, flu, or allergies. It can make our nose itchy and cause us to sneeze. On the other hand, a stuffy nose occurs when the inside of our nose gets swollen, making it feel blocked. This can lead to symptoms like an itchy roof of the mouth, watery eyes, and even a cough. To help with these symptoms, we should drink lots of fluids, especially water, and get plenty of rest.

LUNGS HEALTH

47 STAY ACTIVE

Having fun and playing outside is not only enjoyable but also great for your lungs. When you play and stay active, your lungs get stronger. They work harder to provide the extra oxygen your muscles need. Regular exercise not only makes your muscles stronger, but it also makes your heart and lungs stronger too. So, let's get moving and have fun while keeping our lungs healthy and strong!

48 SLEEP SUFFICIENTLY

Getting a good night's sleep is important for keeping our lungs healthy. When we sleep for around eight hours every night, it helps our lungs stay strong. Our lungs also love it when we eat healthy foods and drink lots of water. Eating fruits, vegetables, and whole grains gives our lungs the nutrients they need to stay healthy. So let's make sure we get enough sleep and eat nutritious foods to keep our lungs happy and strong!

49 AVOID SMOKING

It's important to keep our lungs healthy by avoiding things that can harm them. One of the most important things we can do is to stay away from smoking and secondhand smoke. Smoking is really bad for our lungs and can cause many problems. Even being around someone who is smoking can be harmful to our lungs. We should also try to avoid things like pollution and chemicals that can hurt our lungs. Let's keep our lungs safe and healthy by saying no to smoking and staying away from things that can harm them!

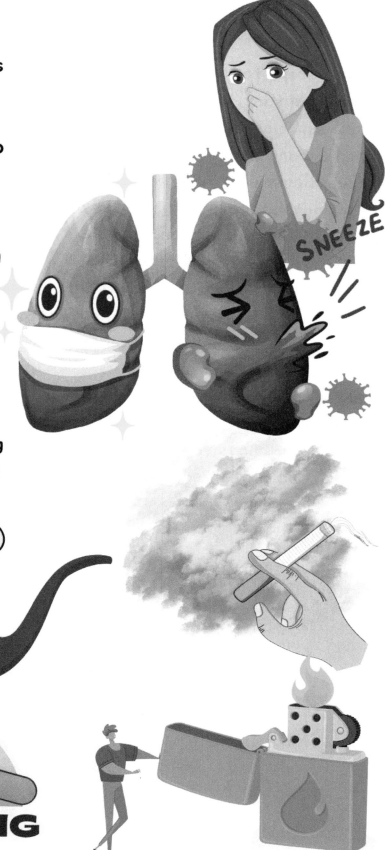

QUIT SMOKING

50 PROTECT YOURSELF

Taking steps to protect our lungs is very important. Wearing a medical mask, especially in crowded places or when around sick people, can help prevent respiratory diseases by stopping dust, pollutants, and viruses from getting into our lungs. Masks were especially helpful during the coronavirus pandemic. Also, getting vaccines, like the flu shot, can protect us from many respiratory diseases. Vaccines work like superheroes, fighting off harmful germs and keeping our lungs healthy. So, let's mask up and get our shots to keep our lungs strong and protected!

LUNGS HEALTH

Circle the lungs-healthy foods.

LUNGS HEALTH

Circle the habits that are healthy for your lungs

RESPIRATORY SYSTEM

Label the parts of respiratory system.

nose	mouth	larynx	trachea	lung	lung

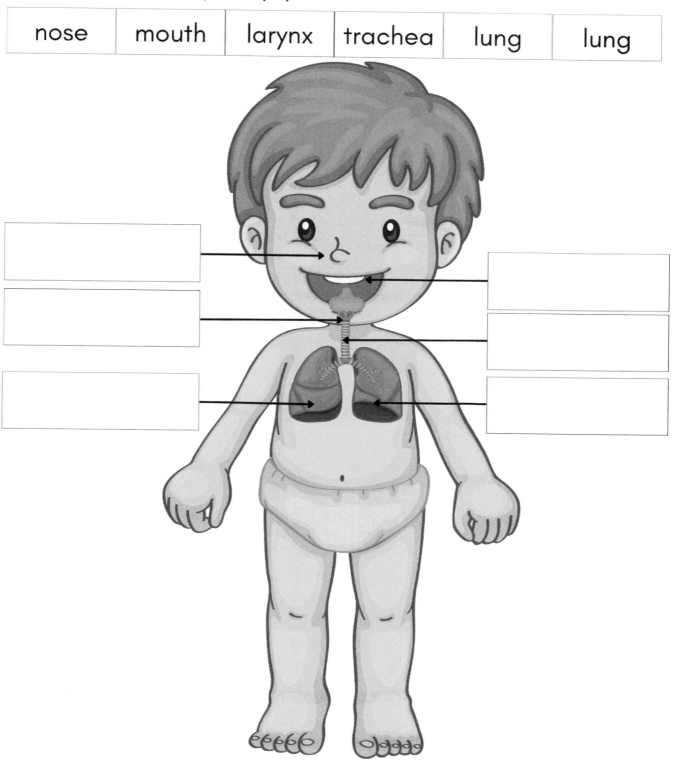

LUNGS HEALTH

Write or draw some tips for keeping your lungs healthy.

BLOOD CIRCULATION

Help the oxygen to find its way to thelungs

51 CAN WE STOP BREATHING

Breathing is something our bodies do automatically, and we can't stop it for a long time even if we try. Our bodies need oxygen to keep all our cells healthy and working. On average, humans can hold their breath for about 30 seconds to 2 minutes. But this time can be different for each person. Factors like smoking, medical conditions, and the health of our lungs can affect how long we can hold our breath. So let's remember to take nice deep breaths and keep our lungs happy and healthy!

52 DIVERS AND ASTRONAUT

In space, astronauts breathe with the help of special equipment that provides them with oxygen. Underwater, divers use tanks filled with oxygen to breathe. Both in space and underwater, humans have found ways to bring the oxygen they need to keep breathing in these unique environments.

53 SPO2 LEVEL

The human body continuously regulates the amount of oxygen in the blood. Low blood oxygen levels can cause damage to important organs such as the brain and heart. It can also indicate that the lungs or heart may not work well. Blood oxygen levels differ from one person to another according to different factors like age, disease, health, breathing rate, and heart or Lung conditions.   The amount of oxygen in blood also known as (SP 02) the normal level is 95% to 100%.

54 THE OXIMETER

There are two main ways to measure blood oxygen levels. We can measure it by a blood draw test that requires a blood sample to measure the levels of oxygen in your blood. This test provides a lot of accurate information.
 Another way to measure (sp o2) at home is using pulse oximetry. A pulse oximeter is a small painless device that is placed on a fingertip. It sends light beams to estimate the oxygen level in the blood.

55 ASTHMA

Asthma is one of the most common respiratory diseases worldwide. It has an effect on the lungs. The airways get narrow, swollen, and blocked by excess mucus. During the attack, the patient's body creates thick mucus that clogs the airways and makes breathing very hard. Some people's allergies can cause an asthma attack. Allergens include things like molds, pollens, dust and pet dander. Smokers have a higher risk of developing asthma

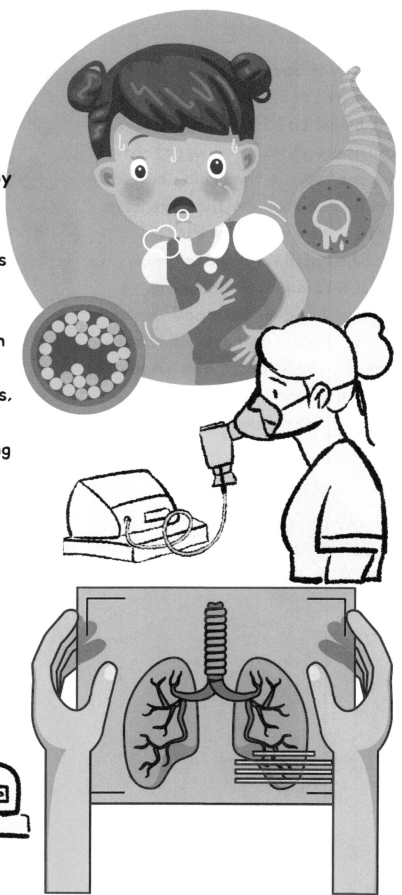

56 THE INHALER

People with asthma usually have common symptoms like chest pain, coughing, shortness of breath, and wheezing (noise sound while breathing). Asthma doesn't go away and it needs ongoing medications to treat these symptoms. The most popular asthma medication is the inhaler. The inhaler delivers the medicine directly to the lungs to relax the muscles around the airways and help the air to move freely. They also let mucus move easily through the airways.

Printed in Great Britain
by Amazon

41422473R00044